PROFESSOR PACKARD'S

DISCOURSE ON THE DEATH OF

WILLIAM SMYTH, D.D.

Wm Smyth.

ADDRESS

ON THE

LIFE AND CHARACTER

OF

WILLIAM SMYTH, D. D.,

LATE PROFESSOR OF MATHEMATICS AND NATURAL PHILOSOPHY
IN BOWDOIN COLLEGE;

DELIVERED BEFORE THE ALUMNI OF THE COLLEGE,

JULY 7, 1868,

BY ALPHEUS S. PACKARD, D. D.

BRUNSWICK:
JOSEPH GRIFFIN.
1868.

BRUNSWICK, APRIL 30, 1868.

PROFESSOR ALPHEUS S. PACKARD, D. D.

MY DEAR SIR;

Arrangements have been made with the Athenæan and Peucinian Societies to waive their usual public exercises on Tuesday afternoon of Commencement week, and I earnestly invite you in the name of the Alumni to deliver before them at that time a Discourse in commemoration of the life and character of our lamented Professor Smyth. From your long association with him and with us, we feel that this would be a peculiarly befitting and acceptable service.

In the belief that such a discourse would be beneficial to many who may not have the privilege of hearing it, and of permanent historical value, I trust you may also be able to furnish a copy for publication.

I am, my dear sir,

Your friend and servant,

J. L. CHAMBERLAIN,

President of the Association of Alumni,
Bowdoin College.

BRUNSWICK, MAY 1, 1868.

GOVERNOR CHAMBERLAIN, LL. D.

MY DEAR SIR;

Your note of yesterday has been received requesting me to deliver a Discourse in commemoration of the life and services of the late Prof. Smyth before the Alumni at the next Commencement. I cannot well decline such a service in memory of the colleague of so many years and a life-long friend, and will endeavor to meet the wishes of my brothers of the Alumni as I best can.

With sincere respect and regard,

Ever yours,

A. S. PACKARD.

BROTHERS ALUMNI:

THE office, which through your President has been laid on me and which under the circumstances I could not well decline, I never anticipated. It never occurred to me, that I remember, that I should be called to bury my life-long friend and colleague. Boys together at Wiscasset, our acquaintance and friendship continued until he entered college, when, as one of the Tutors, I assisted in his examination for admission. A single year passed after his graduation and we were Tutors together, then colleagues in the Professorship. We began married life the same year, 1827, built together the dwelling which was our common home for forty years, our families growing up around us in undisturbed harmony, sympathizing in each others labors, joys, trials and bereavements until the sundering of life-long ties came so suddenly without a moment's premonition. And therefore it is, that the duty of this day seemed to fall upon me, of testifying, so far as

I may, in behalf of the college and the community, to the eminent claims of that steadfast friend, the faithful officer of government and instruction, the citizen of the highest tone of public spirit, and the true man, to the affectionate respect of us all.

It was his expectation, as it was yours, that at this Commencement an important meeting of Alumni would be held, at which he would present a report of what had been done in the work of the Memorial Hall and a new impulse be given to the most signal enterprize yet undertaken by and for our Alma Mater since the corner stone of her first Hall was laid. His report, with his own inspiriting enthusiasm to give it effect, we cannot hear. But, what is more eloquent than any words his living voice could utter, the facts of his life, his works are to speak for him to day. I do not stand before you to eulogize the departed. Happily for us, and for me, a plain simple statement of the facts of his life is such a eulogy as few can receive. Unassuming and with the simplicity of a child, he was emphatically a man of mark here, and would have been any where. No graduate of the forty or more classes that have passed under his instruction but has some distinct recollection and characteristic incident to recall of their instructor. Estimated by what he has done for the college, or the parish, or the town, or for yet wider interests, in teaching, in preparing text-books of the highest class, in efforts and positive labor for the church and religious society of which he was a member, or for the public schools of the State, truly a great life,—a vast amount of self-denying, earnest, honest, whole-souled, energetic, vigorous, noble living has, almost without premonition or warning even to himself, come to its end for this world.

Professor Smyth was born in Pittston, February 2, 1797, in a house now standing on the eastern bank of the Kennebec a mile below the city of Gardiner; but in his childhood his parents removed to Wiscasset which was his home until about the time of his entering college. His father was a mechanic, a ship-carpenter, and at the same time a skilful musician and teacher of music. His mother was of excellent christian life, whose influence in forming his early character he always acknowledged. At the age of eighteen he was bereft of both father and mother and was left with a young sister and brother and nothing but kind friends and himself to depend upon, two other sisters having been otherwise provided for. It was characteristic, as we shall see, of his mind and heart, that during the war of 1812–'15, self-moved and solely to relieve an emergency in the scanty means of his home, he enlisted in the army and gave his bounty money to his mother. He, however, did not serve in the ranks, but was detached by the officer in command at the fort near the mouth of the Kennebec, Col. McCobb, to be his private secretary, and so, as he used sportively to remark, he was a soldier for a year without firing a gun. He would add, that he never in his life discharged a gun, and could not understand the amusement which so many find in sporting.

After his discharge from the army he became a clerk of one of the well known Wiscasset merchants of that day, Hon. Moses Carleton, and a member of his household. His earliest ambition was to qualify himself to teach school. He had no means, and such was his spirit, he would not be dependent on others. But, as was always the case with him, where there is a will, there is a way. Many an hour was spent by him, after his day's work was done, in rather a stealthy way, often stretched on the floor in the light of the kitchen fire brightened now and then by pitch-pine knots, sometimes on the grass under the light of the moon, studying for that to him high aim. Stealthily I say, for, as was characteristic, he was shy of its being known that he had such aspirations. Before those days, in lack of better opportunities, when sent to the ship-yard for chips he would carry his book with him and, at resting places, would put it on his basket or barrow and study his school lesson; or at his father's work-bench would fasten it open on the wall before him, so that, as he plied his tools, he could catch a look at it, and commit to memory or master what he was studying. An incident may be related as showing the early developement of his persevering, resolute spirit. When he was fourteen, a sister was twenty miles away on a visit, and he was sent on horseback to bring her home behind him, a common fashion of riding at that day. He had scarcely ever mounted a horse. The boy was up betimes for his journey, and accomplished it in good time; but the sister had met with an accident to the arm which she would need to cling to her brother on the horse, and it was decided that he must return without her. He thought of the spelling-match which was to be the last school exercise of the day. He was at the head, and if by absence he should forfeit his standing, there were good spellers in the class and it would cost him a struggle to regain his position. He resolved to return without delay, and after a lunch for himself and a brief bating for his horse posted back, accomplishing his forty miles for that day's work, and was in his place in time for the spelling. The boy kept the head at some risk of his own head, and for some days had painful reminders of his achievement.

That first ambition, of which I have spoken, was soon attained and young Smyth gave out modest proposals for a private school. Mr. Carleton, whose mercantile business had been ruined by the non-intercourse and embargo measures and by the war, allowed him the use of his large counting room, now deserted, for this purpose.

But now three or four of his village acquaintance had gone to college, and thus a new and higher ambition was awakened in his susceptible nature. The idea got lodgment in his mind that he too must go to college, and at once he began a new work. Gathering text-books as he could, he commenced the study of Latin and Greek. Without a regular teacher—he never had one in his work of preparation—asking help of boys more advanced in the study, (the late Rev. Charles Packard, then a member of college, used to boast somewhat, it may be, that he gave Prof. Smyth his first lessons in Latin; and I can recall instances of being posed in my own college vacations with questions on obscure passages in the Herodotus of the Græca Majora,) he prosecuted the now all absorbing object of his life, *fitting for college.* After his day's teaching and in his school-room he would work far into the night on his Latin and Greek; often, as he has told me, walking up from that counting room on the wharf through the Wiscasset street at two in the morning to his bed at Mr. Carleton's. To add to his burden of care and anxiety after the loss of his parents, the young sister and brother, already referred to, must, as he felt, be looked after. His characteristic independence of spirit and heroic self-reliance would not allow them to be a burden even on the kindest friends; and he rented a house, still standing on the southern side of Wiscasset Point looking out upon that beautiful bay, himself and these two children constituting the little household. And so he kept school; soon, however, under the enlarged convenience of a more commodious apartment in what had been the Brooks' Hotel, and then again in the brick Academy—a school which had a name in the town for thorough teaching and discipline; at odd hours by day studying for college far into the night, and all the while overseeing the needs of his little household even to their weekly washing with his own hands. But those studies by firelight and by moonlight, and those long evenings subsequently with Greek, came near ruining his eyes and caused him years of trouble.

In 1817 he was brought to the notice of Rev. Reuben Nason, (Harv. 1802) Principal of the Academy at Gorham, Me., a superior classical and mathematical scholar, who needed an assistant; and, though he had employed recent graduates for the position, he ventured to take young Smyth to fill the vacancy, who fully met the demands of the situation and always regarded it a kind Providence that directed his steps thither. He remained with Mr. Nason a member of his family nearly two years, doing his duty faithfully and efficiently as a teacher, hard at work all the time on his Greek and Latin and Mathematics under the most competent council and aid, so far as needed, of his excellent friend, and winning the high esteem and respect of that superior scholar who used to speak of young Smyth as his Greek giant. For the tastes of the student were decidedly for Greek. It was several years before he detected in himself any peculiar turn for mathematical science.

He at length attained his second object of ambition and entered Bowdoin College in Junior standing September 1820. Such an example of student-life as was then to be exhibited is rare and worthy of record. It may encourage some toiling, heart-sick one, who may imagine his lot to be peculiarly hard, and is tempted to give up in despair, to hear of the efforts and self-denials of one of a former generation on these grounds, under the shadow of these Halls and these pines, for an education now worth much more than it was then. He occupied with a townsman and classmate, Boynton, a room in the building, afterwards burnt down, which stood on the sight of Mr. Henry C. Martin's residence opposite the College Halls. I have referred to the serious injury done to his eyes by those firelight and moonlight studies and long evenings over Greek and Latin. Through college he was compelled to wear a green shade and to study by another's eyes. His room-mate read his lessons to him, he occasionally raising his blinder to glance for a moment at a Mathematical formula or a diagram or a phrase. What all students would regard as a grievious misfortune and trial he used to speak of as probably an advantage in one respect, as it contributed to form in him habits of abstraction and concentration, for which he was so remarkable and in which much of his strength lay.

After getting settled in college life the independent, self-denying spirit of which I have spoken led him to bring to his side the young brother and sustain both as he might. This self-sacrificing college student often deprived himself of a dinner for the sake of that brother; lived day after day on bread and water; not unfrequently did not know one day where the next day's meals were to come from; and thus, studying with the eyes of another, often at his wits' end for support, with that care of the brother upon him part of the time, he soon took the lead of an able class and held it to the end, graduating with the English valedictory in 1822.

It ought to be distinctly understood, that Professor Smyth was unusually reticent about himself, his feelings, or experiences, or his personal history. Some of these particulars no living person has heard him refer to. Some of them I myself knew, or remember distinctly as reported at the time; some I have heard him rather incidentally mention. He rarely referred to himself. He left not a scrap of autobiography, though urged to do it by his children. What he did for himself or friends or for the public good he did for the sake of the object, not to be seen or talked of.

After graduating, Mr. Smyth taught a school for a short time in what used to be called Pres. Allen's Academy, designed to be preparatory for the college, a gothic structure near the site of the dwelling which stands next to Capt. Samuel Skolfield's, south westerly from the college yard. He then spent a year in the Andover Seminary, throwing all his enthusiasm into the study of the Hebrew and the Greek of the New Testament under the eminent Prof. Stuart. In 1823 he received an appointment from his Alma Mater as Proctor and Instructer in Greek; then became Tutor in Mathematics and Natural Philosophy; in 1825 adjunct Professor in Mathematics and Natural Philosophy, and so his life's work began.

It has been already remarked, that his predilection was for Greek. When he came to be a teacher in that branch, nothing could have been more to his taste. He loved Greek, and has since confessed to friends a sort of regret that he accepted the offer which consecrated his life to mathematical science and that he had not adhered to his first love. In truth, we may say, it was almost an accident that revealed to himself, as well as to others, the peculiar talent and power, genius it may be called, which has given him so much of a name and reflected so much reputation on the college. His success, as a Tutor of Algebra, quite unexampled with us, led to the somewhat singular application to him of a large representation of a college class who had completed their usual course in Algebra the year before, to hear an extra recitation in that branch with the black-board which he had first introduced into the recitation room. Quite an enthusiasm was excited for a study not apt to be popular, was reported of by students wherever they went, and thus was made known the eminently fit person to relieve Prof. Cleaveland, (who from the opening of the college had been sole Professor in that department and for several years had added to his charge Chemistry and Mineralogy,) of part of his duties, and one who, as an author in Mathematical Science, was to win a name known extensively in our own country and in other lands. In 1828 Mr. Smyth became Professor in full of Mathematics and Natural Philosophy and devoted himself with his peculiar ardor to a branch which, as we have said, came unsought into his hands.

Reference has been made already to the enthusiasm of his nature and his unusual power of concentration. His mind was quick to kindle and his powers to arouse themselves to seize on some engrossing subject, and, while the occasion demanded, he was *totus in illis*. As soon as he came to the chair of his department he set about studying the French systems. He read and mastered the Mécanique Céleste, and his private manuscript will show formulæ which he carefully elaborated while that great work was in hand. At that time it was quite an achievement, I think, it being stated that but three or four individuals in our country had accomplished it. A somewhat amusing instance of his power of concentration I recall to mind. An occasion of some disturbance had required the intervention of the College authorities. At a late hour they returned harried and wearied to their homes and needed rest. The next morning he told me, that before he took his bed he went into his study and took a turn at the Mécanique Céleste which composed his nerves and ensured him a good night's sleep.

As the result of these studies he soon set himself to the work of supplying a need which he felt of text-books for his classes, and, as the first fruits, issued a small work on Plane Trigonometry, availing himself of the ingenuity of the late Mr. L. T. Jackson of this town in preparing blocks on a novel plan for striking off the diagrams. The first edition of his Algebra from the press of Mr. Griffin of this town appeared in 1830, which first adapted the best French methods to the American mind, received warm commendation from Dr. Bowditch, and was adopted as a text-book at Harvard and other Institutions. It passed through several editions and then gave place to two separate works, the Elementary and the larger Algebra. Then followed an enlarged edition of the Trigonometry and its applications to Surveying and Navigation, and treatises on Analytic Geometry, and on the Calculus, the last being so clearly and satisfactorily developed and with so much originality as to receive emphatic approval in high quarters, particularly from the late Prof. Bache, and constituting, it has been said, quite an era in the means of instruction in this profound and, as heretofore reputed, difficult branch. And all this, while he was hearing two, often even three, recitations a day, besides preparing and delivering Lectures on Natural Philosophy and more recently, on Astronomy. His classes will remember the interest of his Lectures on Steam. Cyrus Hamlin (of the class of 1834,) now Rev. Dr. Hamlin of Constantinople, spent his long winter college vacation in constructing with his own hands a small locomotive, which the college added to its apparatus, and which the Professor has constantly used to illustrate the subject with pleasing effect. Those who have heard these Lectures, as well as those on Astronomy, have testified to their interest and value. Beside being scientific, they were discursive in a proper degree, sometimes eloquent, always earnest and instructive.

"I wish I was not so much a man of one idea"! he often exclaimed when he came back from the village street without doing his errand, or left the day's mail where he happened to have called on his way. And so he was in the less common application of the phrase, which was one result of his power of abstraction. Whatever subject of high interest got possession of his mind, if it did not refuse admission to any other claimant on his attention for the time, it was abstracted and distant towards it. It was in some respects his misfortune, the absorbing interest of some one matter engrossing his thoughts and activities to the neglect of whatever else he happened to have in hand. His recitations on this account were perhaps shortened; or in some other way we could detect that his mind and interest were engaged elsewhere. But no one that knew him ever attached to his conception of Prof. Smyth the thought, that he was a man of but one idea in the ordinary sense of the expression.

For thirty years at least he bent his efforts to the main work of his life; and yet all along his toilsome path were by-ways of deep moral, or social, or public interest, often of positive self-denying labor, which drew him aside. He was a whole-souled, large-hearted man. Personal interests occupied with him an inferior place. Had it not been so, he would have accumulated competency from his published works, whereas, had that been his only resource, the fruits of his years of labor would have left but a pittance for his children. To add to the lack of what may have been the best management for his own interest, he lost the stereotype plates of the more important of them in the Portland fire of 1866.

But any real object of philanthropy, of national or of town interest, any thing that touched the life of the College, was sure to find one mind and heart ready to respond to its demands. Some recall how his enthusiasm was fired by the bloody, but fruitless, struggles of the Poles for national life; how eagerly he watched the progress of the conflict, seeking for the best maps to detect their stragetical movements, making himself familiar with every phase, political or military, of the unequal contest and with the name and qualities of the leaders. Then his deepest sympathy was awakened in the Hungarian revolt and its disastrous and ignominious result. The case of the Cherokees and their compelled removal from their own lands, in its turn, enlisted his feelings, not in its paltry aspects as a political question, but as a question of right and wrong involving high principles of national justice and honor. In the late civil war during the operations of the national forces on Missionary Ridge and the vicinity in Georgia, he could not help thinking of the retribution which a righteous Providence seemed to be visiting on a people who were the means of inflicting on a poor Indian nation, just immerging into civilized life through the instrumentality of christian missionaries, a grievous wrong and outrage.

Prof. Smyth was among the first members of the Temperance Society formed in this town when Rev. Dr. Justin Edwards promulgated and advocated with so much effect the doctrine of total abstinence from intoxicating drinks. It was indeed one instance of the energy with which he seized on a principle, that at the age of sixteen, when he saw the direful effects of intemperance around him in all classes, he deliberately formed the determination that he would never indulge in a custom which he saw to be the cause of unmingled wretchedness and woe, and adhered steadfastly to this resolution through life.

A debate in the Brunswick Lyceum made of him an anti-slavery man, or rather turned his thoughts to that subject and inspired a sentiment and opinions which he maintained his life through. The claims of the American Colonization Society were made a subject of debate occupying several evenings. Prof. Smyth *happened*, somewhat accidentally as it seemed to me at the time, to take the adverse side of the question. With his accustomed ardor whenever a moral element was involved, he went to the bottom of that subject, reading every thing of importance within reach, whether speech or document, whether foreign or domestic, and came out fully persuaded in his own mind. Henceforward for several years he gave himself with great earnestness to that cause so far as he could do so without neglecting official duty; delivering public addresses sometimes at the risk of public disturbance and outrage. He was Corresponding Secretary of the Maine Anti-Slavery Society and prepared some of the ablest Reports which the cause produced; for a year edited the Semi-monthly Advocate of Freedom printed in this town; and carried on a controversy in the Christian Mirror with Rev. Rufus W. Bailey of South Carolina on the main points at issue. He undoubtedly took high ground on the subject and was deemed by many to be of the extremists, as he was not one to compromise with what he believed to be error or wrong. But it cannot be said of him justly that he could see but one side of a question. In the height of the conflict, with opinions as decided and thorough as any man's, he would not go with some of his brethren in denouncing the American Board of Commissioners because they would not take what was deemed an advanced step in the matter of slavery as involved in some of the Indian Missions, and maintained a controversy in the public papers in defence of the Board with able and adroit champions of the more radical view. Were these articles collected they would make quite a volume and would be a valuable contribution to the anti-slavery literature of the times. He never swerved, no not for an hour, from his allegiance to the cause of human freedom and the rights of man. Though exposed to reproach and annoyances, to hard speeches and harder looks, he was not a man to be deterred from his purpose or to quail in whatever he regarded a matter of right, truth, and duty.

Then came the subject of Public Schools. The method of graded schools for the large Central District of Brunswick was proposed to the inhabitants, and awakened violent opposition from quarters whence opposition to such schemes of public good usually comes. The project soon engaged his earnest co-operation. He was chosen on the Board of Agents successively for seventeen years; most of the time was chairman, and exercised vigilant supervision of the schools. The amount of labor he performed in securing and perfecting the system, in building the large brick school-house for which he furnished the working plans, and in general superintendence, few can conceive; and all, with no other remuneration than the consciousness of rendering an important public service. He took great interest in children and once declared, that he desired no other inscription upon his tombstone than the simple words, "*The Friend of the Children.*" The town owes a tribute of gratitude, respect and love to this friend of its schools and its children. And not this town only, but every town in the State. By personal advocacy of the "graded system" in different towns by public lectures; and yet more before a Committee of the Legislature with a force of argument and earnest, eloquent persuasion, that made some of our Legislators marvel that a College Professor could labor so heartily and so efficiently even for common schools,—he was instrumental in effecting that a particular provision in relation to the schools of the Village District of Brunswick became a general law for the State. Hon. Phinehas Barnes, whom we shall refer to again in this connection, in a letter to the writer states, that he witnessed the presentation of the case before the Committee, and that his argument and appeal in favor of the system was one of the best pieces of reasoning and eloquence he ever heard. Moreover subsequently, when a case was made by those in Brunswick opposed to the graded system in order to test the legality of certain proceedings under the act, and it was carried up to the Supreme Court, Prof. Smyth thoroughly studied the case, searched the legal authorities, drew up a paper containing what seemed to him the principles of public policy involved, and put it into the hands of the counsel for the Board of Agents, Hon. Mr. Barnes, who found it embraced the main points at issue. The opposing counsel was Hon. Samuel Fessenden. Mr. Barnes was successful in the triumphant vindication of the constitutionality of the Act. The memory of Prof. Smyth will be a cherished tradition in the school-history of Brunswick.

He was for many years one of the Trustees of the first Parish fund; and for forty years or more an active member of the Congregational Church and Society in Brunswick. He was for a long period also one of the Parish Assessors or Committee; a teacher in the Sabbath School; ever watchful of the interests of the Church; jealous of its good name; until within a few years uniformly present at its private meetings; and a liberal contributor of his means, often beyond his means, for the support of the institutions of religion and of every good work. When the present church edifice was erected he was the working member of the building committee, giving important counsel in its plan, even to the framing of the building, and constantly supervising the work. When subsequently it was deemed expedient to make a change in the heavy tower of the structure, he furnished the working plans for a spire which for grace and beauty was not surpassed. Indeed mechanics gave him the credit of being a master mechanic and deferred to his judgment and taste in nice points of architecture and construction. None knows the amount of time and labor he expended on this enterprise; and, after its completion, for the convenience and comfort of worshippers, even superintending the care of the furnaces and in other ways invading the sexton's privilege.

We come now to speak of the last public work of Prof. Smyth's life, the measures for erecting a Memorial Hall for the college. No one else was thought of to take this matter in hand. His patriotic spirit, his long-tried devotion to the college, his unsurpassed energy and indomitable resolution, the inspiring enthusiasm of his character, and his mechanical and architectural skill and taste, marked him out as the only man for the occasion. One even most conversant with him and who had most free access to his thoughts, purposes, and plans, can scarcely enumerate the extent of his correspondence on the subject; his journeyings to and fro from Bangor to New York for subscriptions; his long walks in Brunswick and its neighborhood to obtain contributions, to consult mechanics and contractors, or to engage hands for the work; his visits to other towns to examine public buildings in order to ascertain dimensions of buildings reported of well or ill for public speaking, that his own audience-room might not fail in this respect; to inspect quarries of building stone; or his careful study of architectural designs, sketches and plans in the college library; or his personal labor in meditating and drawing plans himself, that architects might readily conceive the idea and object of the proposed structure. For the last two years his mind and thoughts have been intent on what he often said was to be his last labor. Every dollar of the thirty thousand on his subscription book he solicited, and had collected nearly twenty thousand of the amount, in person. Not that he coveted the credit of the work; but such was the man. Had the project been to survey a piece of land, or to set a post by the road-side, when determined upon by competent authority, he would set about it at once, whether a committee were with him or not; more especially in such an enterprise as this, not waiting for others, or thinking of others. His friends sometimes thought it would have been better for him, if not for the cause, if he would invite others to co-operate at least in a part of the labor.

These various activities of Prof. Smyth's busy life were exercised outside of his official relations. The resources of the College have always been so restricted as to impose on its Professors, for the most part, an unusual amount of tutorial duty; for many years three daily recitations, or an equivalent, four days at least in the week; a heavy draft on the Instructors, we may say in passing, but perhaps to the advantage of the style of teaching. If lectures were given they were the result of extra labor. In later years Prof. Smyth heard two daily recitations, and gave experimental lectures as were required by his department. During the last year or two, arrangements were made to relieve him farther, that he might devote himself to the work of the Hall. Still he had his annual course of recitations and lectures in Astronomy, and had completed it just before his death. As before intimated, it is just to say that these calls of public service were felt in the recitation room. His abstracted manner at times made an impression of a mind pre-occupied, so that a student might take advantage of exemption from the usual scrutiny. But let a second experiment be tried of the Professor's abstraction, the experimenter would be likely to find himself at once exposed to an eye which no error or subterfuge could escape, and perhaps uncomfortably exposed to others. Pupils may thus occasionally have suffered loss, but the College doubtless gained by the contribution it freely made to a public interest. Moreover, as years grew upon him it would not be strange if he accommodated himself with less facility to less quick or less diligent pupils. But his ability as a teacher was never called in question. In explanation he was precise, simple, and clear. He had great power of inspiring interest; his own enthusiasm, which often kindled, especially in certain branches of his department, at the blackboard, being communicated to his class. Later classes will carry through life his setting forth of what he termed the "poetry of mathematics," as exemplified in the Calculus.

As an officer of government he was energetic, fearless, and resolute; decided, though often moderate in counsel, and unwavering under severest trials of firmness. Pupils seldom ventured to trifle with him. He had great power of rebuke and command, and often by a sharp turn or a stroke of wit restored good humor. His fertility of resource availed him in defeating the most ingenious devices for interrupting or evading a recitation. It is thought that no combination ever gained an advantage over him. He always gave an impression of reserved power. College officers experience fluctuations in the favor of their pupils; but no one probably is remembered with more universal interest or ever has been greeted with more cordiality by the Alumni than Prof. Smyth. Every graduate knew his devotion to our Alma Mater. It was earnest, constant, and self-sacrificing. Jealous of its reputation and honor he was vigilant and active in promoting its welfare. His daily prayer ascended in its behalf; he contributed according to his ability to its pecuniary relief; he was active in improvements of the college premises, laying out avenues and planting trees with his own hands. We cannot but think that in his last work for it his life was the sacrifice; for few can know, as we have said, his various and exhausting labors during the last two years. He repeatedly declared that had he foreseen the anxiety and labor which it would cost, he would not have undertaken it. Were the spirit which animated him to pervade the body of alumni, not only would the Hall at once arise to grace the college grounds, but other pressing needs of the College be speedily satisfied.

I have only to add to the enumeration of Prof. Smyth's various public services, that until within two years he was Treasurer of the Me. Branch of the Am. Education Society, almost, I think, from its establishment; and was thus brought into contact with a large number of young men with whom his own experience had taught him to sympathize, and who always regarded him as a friend in need.

Such were the prominent activities in the remarkable life that has now passed away. It only remains to indicate the leading intellectual and moral traits of character which marked the man who has moved and acted among us these forty-five years; and this does not demand special elaboration or particularly nice discrimination, since the absence of concealment or simulation in him was so entire, that he was seen and read of all that had to do with him.

Of the qualities of his mind no one conversant with him could doubt that his Creator endowed him with a power of intense application, of wide compass and great clearness of thought, of strong grasp of principles, and of exhibiting truth, often massive truth, with great precision and force. He had a peculiar faculty of seizing on the salient points and the fundamental elements of any subject he approached.

One could not but give him the credit of childlike simplicity. He was simple in his tastes, in his manners, and in his desires. There was no pretence or affectation in his nature. Better had it been for him sometimes, it may be, if he could have masked or concealed his feelings. Who did not know where or how he would stand on any question of college life, or of the day? Who was not sure that he spake what he meant and meant what he spake? His influence was always for the real in things, and has been a most valuable lesson of life for those who came under its power. No charge of insincerity or false-heartedness was ever laid upon him.

One could not be long associated with Prof. Smyth without discovering that, when aroused, he was a man thoroughly in earnest. The account we have given of him has been from childhood to his last hour an exemplification of the deep earnestness and enthusiasm of his nature. It brought out of him an amount of work both of body and mind of which the world affords rare instances; an example to be commended to young men of one great element of success in life's work.

Those who were connected with Prof. Smyth in social life had abundant proofs of his profoundly sympathetic nature. They cannot forget when the daughter of a brother Professor was prostrated, as was feared, by fatal disease, how his sympathies were stirred, as if she had been his own child; how he watched for her and over her, almost taking the place of a nurse. Neighbors did not live long by him without delicate, considerate manifestations of tender care and solicitude. In his own household his love "was wonderful, passing the love of women." How with all the persistence of his strong nature he contended with disease which within these few years has invaded his family; ransacking the medical library for authorities, studying cases until Medical Professors came to the conclusion that he understood them as well if not better than themselves; and when all was in vain, how the strong man was shaken, though submissive as a child under the blow! He bore with him to his grave the anguish of those sorrows. We who knew him best thought the care of the Memorial Hall was a merciful provision for his relief in those troubles, as it gave him an engrossing object for his mind to work upon. But the dark shadow scarcely ever lifted. A few minutes before he expired, referring to the distress he felt, he said: "It is hard to bear pain, but how much more that dear child (his daughter) had to bear."

During the war of the Rebellion news came of the battle at Chickamauga, and soon after, tidings that a son was on that bloody field; then that he had fallen. All appliances of telegraph and mail were employed to ascertain the truth. Assurance, doubly sure, seemed to come at last that he would never see that son again, and by the same mail which brought a few lines from the son himself, announcing that he was taken prisoner in the battle, and was then in the Libby prison. But the anxieties, the suspense and agony of those days! It seemed as if it would kill him.

The facts of Prof. Smyth's life reveal most clearly a singular self-sacrificing spirit. What reward or remuneration, what personal advantage could he have expected from his labors for schools, or for the church, or for the Memorial Hall? What self-interest could have prompted him to furnish working plans for school-house or church-spire; or to rise from his bed and go down to the school-house in a drenching storm to see that the rain did not undermine the wall or flood the cellar; or at midnight in a driving southeaster to go over to the church then in building, to make more fast an ill-secured transept window; or to serve as a tender to the mason who was putting up a chimney in the tower? I asked him why he did not hire a man to do that work. He replied, he thought it easier to do the work himself than to go over the village to find a suitable hand for it. Or within this year, what gain to himself in walking two or three miles twice the same day, to see a man he wished to employ in some stone work for the foundation of the Hall; and then in other directions, as far, or farther, to inspect quarries of stone! I asked him why in the world he did not hire a conveyance. The answer was, he did not wish to abridge the memorial fund a single dollar.

Another element in the character of Prof. Smyth was true magnanimity of spirit. One like him, a man of strict views of discipline in school or college, of decided opinions and fearless, determined spirit, could not pass through life without encountering opposition, sometimes ill temper or even outrage. But he never harbored resentment, or remembered injuries. The excitement of conflict passed over his spirit and left no ripple behind.

I may add that he was blessed with a genial, buoyant spirit. He never betrayed a moody or sullen temper. There was in him a vein of fine humor. He enjoyed it in others, and no one could turn a witticism or convey a compliment with more delicacy or grace.

It remains to bear testimony to Prof. Smyth as a christian man. In this character he left the record of nearly fifty years in his daily life, in the free intercourse of friends, in the social meetings of the church, in college halls, in his relations to public philanthropic movements of his time, and in the pulpit of the sanctuary. He came to experience the power of religious faith and hope while an assistant in Gorham Academy under the faithful and heart-searching ministrations of Rev. Asa Rand. He once communicated to me something of his experiences at that time, from which of Rev. Asa Rand. He once communicated to me something of his experiences at that time, from which I judged that a deep and thorough work of divine grace was wrought in his heart. When under conviction of his sinfulness and ruin at the preaching of the word, as he once told me, in his characteristic simplicity and honest dealing with himself, he felt as if the preacher was aiming at him personally; and as he went home from the sanctuary he felt that others must know that he had been the subject of the discourse. He was abashed and shy and walked by the roadside to avoid public notice. He then suffered from such mental distress as one of his strong nature may experience, until he fell sick of a typhoid fever. He was brought down to the gates of death; for hours was thought to be dying; but at length was raised to health. As new life was gradually restored, his anxieties concerning his religious state were revived and he passed through a severe conflict, as we have been informed by one who had the best opportunity to know the circumstances. In the depth of his mental distress and darkness, his friend, Rev. Mr. Nason, sat with him a whole night endeavoring to quiet the anxious inquirer. With the morning light (as this friend writes,) his darkness was dispelled and hope and joy beamed upon him; the garment of praise was given him for the spirit of heaviness. He seldom spoke of his personal religious experiences. He never had exstatic joys or peculiarly buoyant hopes. He once declared that he anticipated his sun might go down in a cloud. At the outset, however, he took his stand as a christian young man and became connected with the Congregational Church in Gorham. He seized with the strong grasp of his intellect and heart on what are termed the doctrines of grace. It was at the time when the religious controversy between Drs. Woods and Ware was attracting the attention of the christian public, and he was led by his discussions with a gentleman with whom he boarded, while he kept a winter school, to study and ponder over the points at issue and defend what he regarded to be the truth. He entered college as a christian young man, and always, as an undergraduate, adorned his christian profession. His design and expectation being to enter the christian ministry, after graduation he spent a year at the Andover Seminary. But Providence otherwise ordered. In 1825, however, he received license from the Cumberland Association, and for several years preached with acceptance in Brunswick and neighboring towns. Of late years he has, with rare exceptions, declined this service, chiefly on account of his want of voice. Many can remember his discourses as marked by weighty thought, clear exhibition of truth, simplicity and vigor of style, and earnest and eloquent enforcement of the motives of the gospel and the issues of life and death.

Of later years it has been plain to all that observed him, that the heavy discipline of domestic bereavement and sorrow has tempered and deepened his tone of piety. None but those intimately associated with him knew how bitter a cup of affliction he drained to its dregs. It was affecting to witness the childlike submission of his spirit in family prayer, in which he never failed to make mention of his children in their dispersion, of all afflicted ones, of the College, the Church, the Nation, a world in sin, of the rest which remains, and the glories of God's everlasting kingdom of blessedness and joy. Not long before his departure he was heard, when walking the room by himself, humming the hymn, "Nearer, my God, to thee, nearer to thee." He requested a member of his family, in her morning care of the sitting-room, always to leave the bible on the mantel, that when he came in wearied from his work he might have it at hand to take down and read as he sat by the fireside. Among his last sabbath readings was Pilgrim's Progress, particularly the closing chapters of that wonderful allegory; and his mind was deeply interested and impressed by the scene of Standfast crossing the river. And here was another Standfast in actual life, himself so soon to receive his summons to cross the river!

Repeatedly within the year he spoke of his day of labor as drawing to its close; often expressed a doubt whether he should see the last great work of his life completed; and often said, that he should not live to enjoy the new Hall, though his eyes might be gladdened by the sight of its majestic proportions and its attractive interior and appointments. His last morning, a gentleman from another college called at an early hour upon him and spent some time in inspecting the plans of the Hall and in conferring with him on the acoustic properties of the proposed audience room. At eleven he went out on the ground to meet a contractor with reference to the foundation work, and was there seized with severe distress in the breast, faltered and sat down, pale and ill. The man observed it and told him he ought to go home at once, offering him assistance, which he however declined. With great difficulty he reached home, and staggering with help from one of the family to a lounge threw himself upon it. After such applications as could be devised he seemed to be relieved; but remarked that he believed his work was nearly done. He expressed a doubt whether he should be able to take the afternoon train for Lewiston, whither he had arranged to go to inspect a Hall with a view to its dimensions. He soon came to the conclusion to go to his chamber and his bed. He walked up stairs unassisted, but at the top told his son, who was at his side, to hasten as his strength was fast failing. As soon as possible he threw himself into the bed; seemed to revive, told his son that he wished he would go for the afternoon's mail and to get a liniment for his pain in the chest. There were indications, that within a few days he had been using a liniment, though no explanation would he give for what purpose. The son left the room for a few moments; he was heard to breath heavily; they hurried to his side; he was unconscious, his eyes were fixed, and he expired.

His work was indeed done;—a life-work; scarcely with intervals, almost without vacations, as he often said. Yes, done, so far as his living, active, present energy is involved. But his work lives. He helped to lay foundations. The influence of such as he, and in his position, lives through generations. The work is done and the workman has gone to be seen no more. Fellow teachers, brothers Alumni, Students, let us renew our diligence, each in his work, for are we not taught that we know not when the master will call, whether at midnight, at the cock-crowing, or in the morning?

A STUDY

OF

The Rural Schools of Maine

BY THE

State Superintendent of Common Schools.

1895.

STATE OF MAINE.

EDUCATIONAL DEPARTMENT,
Augusta, August 1, 1896.

The authorized edition of the Report of this department, for 1895, is exhausted. There have been so many calls for that portion of the report describing the condition of the rural schools that it has been decided to issue these pages of the volume in pamphlet form for distribution among the teachers and patrons of the public schools of the State.

W. W. STETSON,
State Superintendent of Common Schools.

A UNIQUE EXAMPLE OF INTERIOR DECORATION.

The rough, bare, unplastered walls changed to an attractive room by ornaments furnished by the good taste and deft fingers of teacher and pupils.

VISITS TO RURAL SCHOOLS.

GENERAL STATEMENTS.

During the summer and fall of 1895 the state superintendent visited two hundred rural schools in eight different counties of the State. This tour was undertaken because it is believed that the schools cannot be improved until it is known what they are, and that this knowledge can only be gained by a careful study of the schools themselves. It was felt that no one had a right to pronounce judgment in so important a matter except upon the most reliable testimony.

On the following blank a record was made of the facts learned about each teacher and school visited.

NOTES ON SCHOOLS VISITED.

Date..............................

Name of teacher....................Age.............

Permanent P. O. address..........................

Name of school ....Town ....;County.........

Length of term.....No. enrolled........No. present.....

She has attended Common Schools....terms.

" " " High " .... " Graduated ...

" " " Normal " .... " " ...

" " " Acad'y or Sem'y .... " " ...

" " " College or Un'ty ....years, " ...

" " " other schools........terms, " ...

She has taught in Rural Schools..................terms.

" " " Primary " .... "

" " " Grammar " .... "

" " " Normal " .... "

She has taught in High Schools .... terms.
" " " Academy or Seminary............ "
" " " other schools..................... "
" " " this school...................... "
List of books she has read on Pedagogy ....
....
Names of educational papers and magazines she is reading ..
....
Number of visits by Superintendent.....................
" " S. S. Committee ....
" " parents ....
She is a member of the following educational associations...
....
Number of meetings attended within the year.............
She has attended Summer School..................terms.
How was Reading taught?............................
" Spelling " ....
" Penmanship " ....
" Number " ....
" Geography " ....
" History " ....
" Language " ....
" Physiology " ....
" Book-keeping taught?.......................
" Civics " ....
" Music " ....
" Drawing " ....
" Map Drawing " ....
Number of books in library...........................
Number of papers and magazines in library...............
List of apparatus..
....
Kind of house ....Condition............
" desks.................... " ....
" outhouses .... " ....
" grounds .... " ....

Kind of fences.................. Condition...........
" ventilation .... Value ....
Was the room tidy? ....
Was the room attractive?..........
What has the teacher done in these directions............
....
Strongest point about the teacher ....
Weakest " " " ....
Strongest feature in the work ....
Weakest " " " ....
Does the school pay?............ Why? ....
....
....

It will be noticed that this outline is so complete that two hundred of these documents furnish sufficient data for averages which may be trusted to tell the story as to what the schools are. It is believed that a careful study of so large a number of schools, representing the extreme limits of the State, and including some of the sparsely settled sections, as well as the oldest portions, furnishes facts for a reliable estimate of what the best schools are doing, and of the condition and work of the "poor" schools in different sections of the State.

No attempt will be made in this report to give a detailed statement of the work found in the best schools, nor will extended comments be made on what was seen in the average school that deserved commendation. The statements found in another section of this report must suffice in these particulars. While the general object of these visits was to learn what the schools are, still the particular purpose was to ascertain the facts which would enable the visitor to give a detailed description of those schools in which incompetent teachers were found, and to offer some suggestions as to the methods by which they may be improved. It is to be understood that the criticisms found below apply, in full, only to those schools which are ranked as "poor" or "very poor." They are true only in a limited sense of those which are rated as "fair," "good" or "excellent."

I wish the above paragraph might be re-read each time the reader comes to any new description of poor teaching.

Of the schools visited six per cent. are ranked as "excellent," twenty-one per cent. as "good," thirty-two per cent. as "fair," and forty-one per cent. as "poor" or "very poor." These terms are used to represent the different kinds of schools found and to arrange them in classes so that they may be conveniently referred to in the subsequent portions of this report.

In my comments on the teachers and the work they are doing I wish to say, at the outset, that in point of scholarship, in quality of methods, and in the thoroughness of the work done, I found teachers who compare favorably with those who rank highest in our graded schools. They know the facts they are required to teach and are familiar with the subjects in which they should give instruction. They emphasized the essentials and gave but little time to the non-essentials. They were conversant with the work done in the best schools and it was clear that their methods were the result of reading, study, observation, adoption, adaptation. They possessed unusual energy, strong personality and great power of control. They despatched the details of the work expeditiously and quietly. Their manners indicated culture and breeding. The mental and moral atmosphere of the school was inspiring and wholesome.

The above sentences fairly express my judgment as to these teachers and their work. Having said this much in commendation I feel free to state, with equal frankness, other facts, which I regret it becomes my duty to place in this record. For this report to be of value to the State, or service to the teachers, it must be based on facts which fairly represent the condition of the schools inspected.

It is a matter of some interest to note that no one portion of the State has all of the good schools, and that no one sec-

THE POOREST OF THE PAST.

All cuts in this Report are made from photographs of rural school houses built previous to 1893.

tion is suffering from all the poor schools, but that the good and the poor are about evenly distributed.

Some of the best were discovered in what might properly be called "back districts." It is also true that some, which were ranked as "very poor," were found within a few miles of the larger centers of population. These facts have both their encouraging and discouraging aspects. It is encouraging to know that there are no sections so far in advance of all the others that any need be discouraged by the contrast. It is gratifying to find that some of the best schools are maintained in parts of the State where apparently there are but few things to assist in making a model school.

It is discouraging to know that there are communities in all parts of the State that are so little interested in their children as to be willing to tolerate such teaching as to clearly indicate that parents, teachers, and children are destitute of the desire to have schools which can be of any service to them.

It is as astonishing as it is discouraging to see teachers in our schools who claim to be graduates of institutions of considerable standing, who cannot pronounce familiar words correctly, or give the children any information in regard to matters which come within the range of their observation or experience. They cannot read intelligibly, they cannot speak or write grammatically in continued discourse, and they know comparatively little about the facts contained in the text-books used. In a word, they are grossly and densely ignorant.

Any one who is familiar with school work knows that it is possible for students to graduate from an institution of a high grade and yet be unfit in point of scholarship to take charge of any school. They have neither the capacity nor the desire to master the studies which they have pursued, but by some skill, which would do credit to persons of greater ability, they have worried their way through the course and secured their diplomas, while in point of attainment they are not scholars, in any sense of that term.

It is to be regretted that some of our higher schools are willing to allow students to enter their classes and take the sciences and advanced work in language and mathematics, when the instructors in charge of these institutions know that they have little knowledge of the common English branches.

It is hoped that the time is not far distant when the examinations for admission to our secondary schools will be of such a character as to force candidates to have a reasonable mastery of the studies pursued in the common schools before they are allowed to take this more advanced work. The authorities of these schools should protect themselves and the common schools by insisting upon a rigid examination in the common English branches before students are admitted to their regular courses.

One is shocked to see glaring advertisements of some favorite brand of tobacco in so many of our school-rooms. It is not easy to understand why a teacher is willing, either to bring such pictorial illustrations into her school, or allow them to remain if found there. It is vastly better to leave the walls bare than to have them covered with pictures which will interest children in things about which they should not be thinking, or will place objectional matters in such a light as to give them a tacit approval.

If it is impossible for the teacher to provide pictures of merit she would better not make the mistake of disfiguring the walls of the school-room with advertisements of a questionable character. When reproductions of some of the finest works of art can be bought at a nominal price, the excuse that one cannot obtain good pictures is seldom a legitimate one. The fact that children are so vitally influenced in their tastes, judgments and conduct by things placed before them in a pictorial form justifies one in speaking decidedly on this subject.

The fact that there are so few children in the common schools over thirteen years of age should alarm all who believe that the safety of the republic depends on the education of

THE POOREST OF THE PAST.

the citizen. Eighty-seven per cent. of all the children found in the schools visited were under the age named above. This fact means that children are leaving school at a much younger age than formerly. As far as could be learned, those who have left school are not attending other or higher schools. The tendency to leave school and engage in some work, or waste the time in idleness, is increasing each year. If these tendencies are allowed to control the children, the rural schools will soon be made up of pupils who belong in the primary grades only. The law provides that all persons between five and fifteen years of age shall attend school for at least sixteen weeks each year. It is evident that this law is evaded in a large number of instances. It is not necessary to state that it is of the highest importance that school committees and truant officers see that this law is enforced.

It was gratifying to find some schools with so large an attendance. One school in Cherryfield, Washington county, had seventy-two pupils enrolled and sixty-nine present. In this school there were only ten pupils over thirteen years of age.

The record shows that the average attendance in the schools visited was twenty-one, the average length of the terms was ten weeks and the average age of the pupils was between nine and ten years.

These figures, considered in connection with other facts, indicate that the weakest place in our schools is not in the number attending any one school, but in the fact that pupils leave school before they have had time to acquire the elements of an English education. It is not possible for the average child to so master the subjects taught in our common schools, before he is thirteen years of age, as to give him the education he will need in performing the duties which fall to the lot of the average citizen.

TEACHERS.

The criticisms found in this section of the report are to be understood as applying in full to those teachers who are ranked as "poor" or "very poor."

There is a feeling on the part of some patrons of the public schools that many of the teachers of the State are too young to be able to perform properly the duties devolving upon them. The statistics collected during these visits show that the age of the youngest teacher found in charge of a school was fifteen years, the oldest forty years. The average age was between twenty-four and twenty-five years, and a comparatively small number was found under twenty years of age. These figures make it clear that this criticism on teachers is not well founded.

But the record reveals an educational and professional standard which is to be deplored. Fifty-two per cent. of the teachers visited acquired all the education they have in the common schools. Thirty-eight per cent. have attended academies or seminaries for about one year. Ten per cent. are graduates of normal or training schools, academies, seminaries or high schools of a standard grade. It was disappointing and discouraging to learn that only twenty-three per cent. of the teachers have read or are reading works on teaching, and that about an equal per cent. have read or are reading educational papers or magazines. Less than thirty per cent. are attendants on the meetings of any educational association.

It is not encouraging to have to make record of the fact that ninety-four per cent. of these teachers have taught only in district schools. These figures show a lack of experience that helps to explain many criticisms made on the work done by so large a per cent. of these teachers.

While it is true that some of the teachers who are superior scholars were inferior instructors, it is also true that no teacher was discovered who was deficient in scholarship who was successful as an instructor. In this particular, at least, the theory held by leading educators and the facts as found in the school-room agree. There have been times when people believed if a teacher had muscle enough to subdue the big boys and frighten the small ones, he was fit to teach the average district school, although he might be as innocent of scholarship as his instruction was destitute of usefulness.

It would be impossible to convey to any one, who is not familiar with the facts, a full appreciation of the extent to which some teachers are ignorant of the matter contained in the text-books from which they are supposed to give instruction. But a small number are familiar with subjects outside of the text-books, while those who have an appreciative knowledge of the forms of nature by which they are surrounded, the events or the persons who have made or are making history, are so rarely seen as to attract attention when found.

It is mortifying to the visitor to see so little ability to devise new ways of conducting the recitation, to use new illustrations and explanations, and give a larger and more intelligent view and conception of the lessons.

In not a few schools there was little to indicate that the teacher had any special place of beginning the work, or any reasons for beginning at the place where she did. The lessons were assigned without any apparent thought, attention or care as to the assignment. The recitation, too often, was simply a stupid recital of words in which the teacher did a large part of the work, and the pupils divided the suffering with the visitor. There was little to indicate an assured grasp of the subject discussed, or an intelligent comprehension of the thought expressed. There was no evidence that any method was being used, and in many cases the fact that there is such a thing as a method did not seem to have dawned upon the teacher. One teacher asked what was meant by this word "methods" she heard used so often recently.

A few things have come to be accepted by intelligent people who have attended the public schools, who believe in them and who make a study of their work. It is their decision that no one is fitted to take charge of the education of children who has not mastered the facts which she is expected to teach, and that in addition to this knowledge, professional training and experience are needed to make the best teacher. It is to be regretted that these simple facts, which are so generally known, are so little influential in the selection of teachers. It is passing strange that superintending school committees and superintendents are willing to employ teachers without attempting to ascertain if they have any of this fitness to teach.

It should be understood that the teachers are not entirely to blame for their incompetency. Many of them have been trained in schools of the same character as those they are "keeping;" they have been urged to take charge of schools before they were fitted to do so, and they have been tolerated in school when they and those who employed them knew they were not doing satisfactory work. The attempt to place all this responsibility on the teachers is to do an injustice without helping to correct a serious evil.

The State will have good teachers when parents and school officials demand more preparation for the work and better teaching. As long as superintendents are willing to employ the teacher who will work for the lowest salary, so long will a large number of incompetent teachers be employed. If parents would cordially assist in consolidating schools, these officials would feel justified in paying reasonable salaries, and they would exercise greater care in assuring themselves that the teachers employed are fitted by nature, training and experience to teach a school of a quality that will win the approval of an intelligent and progressive community.

But it is only just to state that all of the incompetent teachers are not to be charged to the common schools. Some who have received all of their training in these schools show a very fair grade of scholarship, while those who have "been through" institutions which are supposed to specially fit them for their work exhibit a lack of knowledge which seems incredible.

The virility of the children is sapped by the practice of so many teachers who are trying to do the work for the children, instead of being willing to think sufficiently to induce the children to do the work themselves. Usually it is a small matter for a teacher to solve a problem and give a crude analysis of the work done, but it is quite a different thing to have the children ask and answer such

THE POOREST OF THE PAST.

questions as will compel them to think out the solution. There is but slight appreciation of the fact that it is a sacred duty which the school owes the pupils to furnish such training as will make it a pleasure for them to work, think, dig.

The visitor is impressed with the extent to which teachers and children fail to appreciate the fact that books talk about real things, about men and women who have lived, forms of nature that surround them and things that have happened. In many schools, books are used in such a way as to warrant the feeling that they treat of a different world, and have to do with something entirely separate and apart from the life and experience of the teacher or the child.

It is pitiful to see the extent to which children are rendered torpid, stupid, incapable of intellectual or emotional activity by being forced to say things which they do not understand, to study and recite technical terms and definitions, which are beyond their comprehension.

The average child cannot think in the language of the average text-book. In spite of this fact, he is required to commit to memory and recite words, year after year, when the recitation means nothing but a slavish grind. The child infers from his experience that what is said in books has nothing whatever to do with the men, or things with which he comes in contact.

It is strange that teachers will permit children to interrupt and render practically useless the recitation, by allowing pupils who should be studying, to ask help in finding answers to the simplest questions in their lessons.

In too many schools there was a stream of pupils from the desks to the teacher, and from the teacher to the desks, asking foolish questions, questions which the children could themselves answer with a little study, and which when answered by the teacher are of no benefit to them whatever.

The extent to which the children are injured by all this blundering is manifest in their lack of the power of application, the ability to study out things unaided by others; and these facts account for their being limp, careless, helpless, heedless.

One is shocked to see the manifestations of boorishness, clownishness, slovenliness, which a teacher will permit in her presence without comment, certainly without reproof. There is but little evidence that the children have yet been inspired to want to do better than they are doing.

One can but be impressed with the frequency with which he hears teachers speaking in loud, shrill, harsh tones, a key much above the natural one, and with a force entirely disproportionate to the demands made upon the voice.

Many teachers are not careful enough in their manners, in their intercourse with the children. Their tone, appearance and carriage are not always creditable to an instructor. They do not seem to realize that their personality may count for much in helping the children to better ideas and ideals of life and living.

PUPILS.

It is difficult to convince the public of the extent of the ignorance of pupils in the schools which are ranked as "poor" or "very poor" about things with which they come in daily contact. One can hardly realize that it is possible for children to cultivate and handle flowers all their lives, to stub their toes every day against rocks, to care for animals regularly, without knowing something about what they are, and having some appreciation of their beauty and usefulness. They are equally ignorant concerning the men and women who have attained distinction in New England. Who they are, what they have done, the character and value of their services, are things which have never come within the range of their reading or instruction. The blank stare which mantles their faces when they are questioned concerning these matters is painful to witness.

In their regular work they are allowed to stumble through sentences of which they have no comprehension, guess at answers and become dazed and lost in a labyrinth of mysteries of which they have but the slightest knowledge. The recitations are vague, blundering, unintelligible, because they are unintelligent attempts to talk about things of which they know but little, in terms of which they know less. That they fail to add to the child's stock of ideas or increase his store of facts is not strange. They have not been trained to see, discriminate, contrast or compare. They cannot speak or write English with facility, correctness or force.

The extent to which teachers permit children to speak in indistinct, drawling, mumbling, hesitating tones is surprising. A large proportion of them close their sentences with the rising inflection, as much as to say, "Have I given the correct answer?" Many of the questions are so worded that the child can answer them by yes or no, and he is often allowed to guess twice on each question.

In many cases the teacher, after asking a question, will state the answer, and ask the pupil if his answer does not agree with hers. It is not necessary to pronounce judgment on such teaching; it condemns itself.

There is not that evidence of self-respect and desire to excel on the part of the children which it was hoped would be seen. They are not only lacking in these things, but they are wanting in grasp, tenacity, power to assimilate thought, and indicate that they have not done the work and carried the responsibility which develop fiber and vigor. They are unwilling to apply themselves and are willing to be dependent upon others. They show a lack of resolution, strength, sturdiness, and are blind and deaf to sights and sentiments of beauty. They are wanting in alertness and accuracy and are deficient in eagerness, enterprise, ambition.

When the visitor looks at the reverse side of the shield, he is impressed with the energetic, wide awake, progressive quality of the children who are found in rural schools which are in charge of competent teachers. They are not always courteous, and are sometimes wanting in thoughtfulness.

They frequently speak in tones that grate on your ears and are not always careful about the way they stand, sit, or walk. They are frequently boisterous, sometimes a little coarse, occasionally rude, but seldom vulgar. Even a brief study of them and their work will convince any one that their eyes are open, that their minds are receptive and acquisitive, and that their hearts and heads are being attuned and trained to see and enjoy beauty in life, literature and art.

It is not necessary to visit many schools to discover that there is no class of people in the State who can be more benefited by physical training, than the children in the country schools. They have to engage in manual labor in such a way as to develop strength of muscle without giving a corresponding ease and grace of movement. Such physical exercises should be given as will enable a child to gain absolute control of his muscles. If a child can do this, he has an advantage over his untrained companion which can be appreciated only by those who have attempted to make their way in the world among men and women of refinement and culture.

There never was a time when grace and ease of movement were not useful. The present makes larger demands in this direction than any previous time. As the children of to-day are to be the men and women of to-morrow, and are to associate more largely with all classes than any previous generation, the importance of this matter cannot be overstated.

The rapid introduction of improved means of transportation will not only permit, but make it necessary for people living in the remotest parts of the State to come into immediate contact and intimate association with people from all parts of the world. To meet these larger requirements satisfactorily the children must get from the common schools something more and something better than they are receiving to-day.

Many children have an unwise and unreasoning ambition. They feel that if they are reading in the sixth reader, reciting from the large geography and struggling with the intricacies of cube root, they are being educated. Many pupils

THE POOREST OF THE PRESENT.

in the rural schools are floundering in these subjects, who should be studying the third reader, mastering fractions and learning the geography of their own State. It is a great mistake to allow children to attempt work which their previous training and present abilities do not fit them to study.

These mistakes account for the unwelcome facts that they are wanting in thoroughness, lacking in application and destitute of the power of comprehension. And much of this disgrace is due to the feeling that the book the children study and not what is learned is the all important matter.

Children must be led to see that it is necessary for them to master the studies assigned to the common school course in order to be fitted for the duties and responsibilities of life; that they must be able to read understandingly, write intelligibly, talk with ease and cipher with certainty; that they must be able to appreciate the beauty and the wisdom of the works of art of some of the masters, whether they be given them in the form of pictures or poems.

It would be unjust to close this section of the report without making record of the fact that in the schools of Northeastern Aroostook the boys and girls are noticeably courteous. Whenever a visitor enters the school-room, the pupils rise in their places, and after bowing, remain standing until a signal from him gives them permission to sit. Whenever and wherever met, outside of the school-room, the boys lifted their hats and the girls courtesied. All these things were done with an ease and grace which show that they inherit the instinct from their parents, and that they have been carefully trained in the home and at school. When the majority of the people of a community are thoughtful and courteous, it is simply yielding to an unconscious impulse that makes the children conform to the forms and usages of good society.

ARITHMETIC.

The work in arithmetic in forty-three per cent. of the schools is characterized by a senseless committing and reciting of rules, and an unreasoning explanation of problems, with little or no attempt to connect this work with the daily experiences of the children. Much of the work consists of puzzles to be guessed, and analyses which were parrot-like recitals of words that would convey as much meaning if their order were reversed.

Too much work is assigned for each lesson. Not enough is done in the way of illustrating, explaining, testing the principles taught. When the lesson is assigned and the words are recited, it is assumed that the work in done. The children are grossly deficient in their knowledge of the four fundamental rules and common and decimal fractions. They do not understand the principles, they cannot apply them and they are lamentably lacking in the ability to perform the processes.

In most of the schools but little time is given to mental arithmetic. The average child is dependent on his book, his pencil and his slate in solving the simplest problems. If he is asked to multiply 25 by 5 he laboriously works out the result on his slate. Teachers fail to understand that at least one-third of the time given to this subject should be devoted to mental arithmetic; that the children during this recitation should not be supplied with books; that the teacher should read the problem, the pupil should repeat it, solve it and give a simple, intelligible analysis, and that during all this time he should rely entirely upon his memory for his facts and his mental processes for his results. Such training will develop the memory and power of concentration, and give speed and accuracy in the work.

In many of the schools but little time is spent on the work which gives the child a clear idea of number and of its simple combinations. But few children are so taught that they know what 1, 2, 3 and 4 are. They do not seem to comprehend their values, or what purposes they serve. The Grubé system of developing the idea of number is used in but few schools. The child is left to think of figures as hieroglyphics the meaning of which it is not a part of his business to know. He stumbles through the fundamental rules and is pulled through fractions without knowing much about them, and passes on to work in percentage and square and cube roots, and with these he struggles and flounders for years. The solution of simple, practical examples which are within his comprehension, and that have to do with his daily life, is a form of work that does not seem to have occurred to the teacher, or come within the experience of the child.

Great changes must be made in this matter of instruction in arithmetic. The work in the four fundamental rules, fractions and the simple application of percentage must be so thoroughly done that the children can add columns of figures as easily as they can read a line of print, perform the combinations as rapidly as they are announced, combine fractions as readily as whole numbers and use percentage as familiarly as they do the addition tables. Parents, teachers and children must come to appreciate the fact that these are the topics in arithmetic for which they will have the greatest use in life, and that from the study of these they can gain as much power as from any part of the subject. When a child has finished arithmetic, he should be able to perform all the combinations with speed and accuracy, he should be able to apply all of the principles learned and formulae given in the ordinary experiences of life, and he should be able to use what he has learned in an intelligent, intelligible manner.

The objects to be sought in teaching arithmetic are the ability to understand and the power to use. The child must first be taught the significance and value of the symbols which he uses, and then he must be so instructed as to be able to combine these readily and accurately.

He should begin to reason as soon as he has acquired a sufficient store of facts and such a mastery of principles as will enable him to derive benefit from the process.

READING.

One realizes what a school is not doing when he hears pupils and teachers saying Edinburg for Edinboro', asslum for asylum, Cy-clees for Cyclades, im-pi'-ous for im'-pi-ous, re'-cess (intermission) for re-cess'. stip-u-lees for stip-ules, ep-i-tome for e-pit'-o-me, es-cen-tric for ec-cen-tric, and so on through a list that might be extended to almost any limit.

Some teachers and most pupils do not know how to use a dictionary. The diacritical marks, the marks of accent and the hyphen are cabalistic symbols which convey no meaning to them. They do not know the names or values of these characters and therefore do not know how to apply them to a given word. They do not seem to realize that the words in a dictionary are arranged according to their spellings. The ability to use a dictionary efficiently is limited to a comparatively small number of the pupils in the public schools, a much smaller number than many people suppose.

In forty-five per cent. of the schools the recitations in reading were exercises in pronouncing words without an intelligent attempt to discover their meaning, beauty or force. The thought, and the skill with which it is expressed, are items which did not seem to interest the children and this conception of reading had not yet dawned upon the teacher. They failed to get ideas from the words, the sentences, or paragraphs. They could not see the pictures painted in poems, the portraits sketched in selections, and there was no appreciation of the richness of the thought of the author. They failed to feel the warm life that throbbed in his words and burned in his sentences. It was a monotonous, profitless grind. The children did not realize that what they were reading had to do with anything which had been, or anything that existed at the present, or anything that was to exist in the future. They seemed to think, so far as they thought at all, that it was something outside of their relations and interests. It did not touch their lives, or any life at any point. It was unsympathetic, want-

THE POOREST OF THE PRESENT.

ing in joy, destitute of human interests. It was dreary, heavy, laborious. It was weariness to the teachers, drudgery to the children and productive of imbecility to both. Some of the masterpieces of English were read in such a way as to give none of the zest, inspiration, breadth of view, range of vision, grasp of thought and inspiring and toning influence which are redolent in these selections.

Children fail to sense things. They do not see the beauty, the force, the impressiveness of the selection studied, or the means used to express them. There are no poems in pictures, no pictures in poems for them. They fail to hear as well as to see.

In some cases children seem to have the power to call words rapidly and easily, without being able to grasp the thought expressed. The ability to convey in their tones some suggestion of the thought which the selection contains is something which they have not realized can be done.

For a teacher to reveal to a pupil the beauties, wisdom and inspiration of literature, she must have an appreciation of and love for literature. Its force, beauty, richness, strength must appeal to her and not appeal in vain. She must possess the artistic instinct, the ability to see and express, and have breadth of vision and power of appreciation. The most the average child needs is simply to be introduced to things, but for an introduction to be of any service, to result in any help to him, it must be given by one who fathoms the thing introduced.

It is the silent, subtle, immaterial quality of the teacher that is most influential with the child. It is this quality which moulds, guides and controls him long after the teacher has ceased to instruct. These are the things that are hardest to put into words, but are most potent in life.

LANGUAGE.

It is difficult to describe the work done in Language in the schools classed as "poor," or "very poor." As far as could be ascertained the efforts of the teacher were limited to asking the questions found in the book and listening to recitals of the words of the text. The extent of the work was narrower than the book used. There was little or no attempt made to have the children talk about the subjects studied. Incorrect forms of speech used by the children did not attract the attention of the teacher, at least, no attempt was made to correct them, and the knowledge of the pupils in this subject did not make it possible for them to tell in what the errors of a faulty construction consisted, nor enable them to give the correct form. The study period was evidently devoted to memorizing definitions and rules.

That this study should assist the pupils in enlarging their vocabularies, or help them in the correct use of language did not seem to be thought of. The pupils were not asked to talk, or write about things of which they had some definite knowledge. No attempt was made to reveal to them the force, beauty, or peculiar meaning of words. As a rule, words were not subjects for study, but symbols, the value of which they sometimes understood, but more frequently did not. Sentences were collections of words the significance and force of which they sometimes realized, but usually failed to apprehend.

The work in grammar failed to assist the children in writing and speaking in continuous sentences with ease, force and propriety. Much of the written and oral work was characterized by elliptical, ungrammatical and meaningless sentences. It was not definite, accurate, helpful, nor did it train the children in the fine choice of words, happy forms of expression, and striking sentences which characterize clear thinking, interesting talking and attractive writing. The time was almost entirely devoted to a study about language instead of practice in language. The meagerness of the children's vocabularies was painful to witness. They knew but few words and these they seemed to know more through an act of the memory than through any proper comprehension of their meaning.

This subject can never be taught successfully unless the teacher is able to select the root, prefix and suffix of words, and give the meaning of each and combine them in such a way as to express the thought which the word conveys. The children must be so directed and assisted in their observations of and talks about things that they will develop the ability to see, know and express, in the happiest way, the idea which their study has given them. It takes years of training to fit one to select and arrange the words which will clearly described and forcibly voice the thing seen, heard, or thought by the speaker. In its written form more attention must be given, not only to the construction of the sentence, but to its mechanical features. Indenting and paragraphing, the use of capital letters and marks of punctuation should be taught, by having the children use them properly in all their written work. When pupils are prepared for the high school they should be able to talk and write intelligently about any subject of which they have an accurate knowledge.

The best work in language will be done when it is taught in every grade, in every recitation during the entire course; when all lessons are lessons in language; when the teacher uses correct and vigorous English, and is able to train the children to do likewise.

There is, in the common schools, no study which yields so slight a return for the time devoted to it as the subject of grammar. It is often disliked by the pupils, dreaded by the teacher and frequently a mortification to the visitor. If it is ever to be raised to the plane it should occupy, the teacher must fit herself thoroughly for the work and must help the children to such a command of language as comes only from observation, reading, study, practice.

GEOGRAPHY.

The most of the time devoted to geography is spent in learning the location of small towns, insignificant rivers and unimportant mountains, capes, bays, etc. Much time is given to the geography of Africa and Asia and the Islands of the Sea. But few teachers make any use of the fact that the most of the physical phenomena of the world are found within the immediate vicinity of the school-rooms in which they teach. To make a diagram of the school-room, a picture of the school-house, a map of the school yard, town and county has not yet occurred to the average teacher. But few teachers make a careful study of the location of the objects in the school-room, school-house and school yard. Children read, talk and recite about islands, lakes rivers and mountains, without realizing what these things are, or discovering that they have in their immediate vicinity small islands, tiny rivers and low hills.

The teacher should make a careful study of the boundaries of the town in which she is teaching, its physical features, the industries followed by the people, the places of note or interest, and all those items which go to make up the history and present condition of the community. The school-room is an epitome of the town, the town of the county, the county of the state and the state of the nation. The county and state should be studied in the same general way as the town has been. These should be followed by a careful study of the United States and Europe, and then something should be learned of the general features of Africa and Asia.

Beginning at home lead the children to learn about things in the vicinity of the school, then aid them in getting adequate ideas of things at a distance. By this plan they will be able to understand and appreciate what they study, because they will have something at hand with which they may compare, contrast and measure the thing studied.

HISTORY.

A large part of the time devoted to the study of history is given to committing to memory unimportant dates and describing and locating unimportant events. History is taught in such a way that children fail to comprehend that it

THE AVERAGE OF THE PRESENT.

is simply a record of past efforts. They somehow get the idea that the men who have lived, the things that have been done, belong to another and a different world. They do not understand that we are making history in the present, that it does not deal entirely with the past. Too much time is given to details, and not enough to studying great events—the causes producing them and the results flowing from them. None of the teachers seemed to have made a careful study of the men who have given color to history. Who they were, who their ancestors were, when they were born, where they were born, the schools they attended, the experiences through which they passed, their vocations, their avocations, the influence which they exerted, the things they have tried to do and failed to do, the things they have succeeded in doing; their quality, character, personality, strength, weaknesses; their talent, genius; the ways in which they have served the world, the ways in which they have injured the world, occupy but little of their time and less of their thought.

If one knows the great events and great men of the past, he is able to stand upon mountains from whose summits he can survey the surrounding country. The details will cluster around these men and these events so that he can see the genesis, the relations, the harmony, the progress of history; he can see where we started, along what roads we have come, what point we have reached and in what direction we are going.

When studied in this way history means something, says something. It becomes an inspiration, an aspiration. It develops, it strengthens, it moulds, it purifies. Taught in the usual way it is dwarfing, benumbing, stupefying; it gives the children false ideas of men, wrong ideas of events and paralyzes where it should inspire. To teach history in this better way the teacher must have a love for, an appreciation of the subject. She must know something more than a list of dates, a catalogue of names, an outline of events. She must know something of the philosophy and range of history; in a word, she must have the instincts of the historian.

SPELLING AND PENMANSHIP.

It is very gratifying to be able to state that the work in oral and written spelling and penmanship was fairly creditable, when the ages and training of the pupils are taken into consideration. This statement contradicts the accepted theories concerning these two studies.

BOOKS AND MATERIAL FOR SUPPLEMENTARY WORK.

Of the schools visited but a small number were supplied with books for supplementary work in any of the studies. It cannot fairly be said that any of the schools had a sufficient collection of books to justify one in dignifying it by the name of a library. It is to be regretted that not a single school of all those visited was supplied, or had supplied itself, with papers or magazines for the pupils to read in connection with their regular work.

About ninety per cent. of the schools were supplied with maps, some of them of recent issue, most of them so old as to be practically valueless. About fifty per cent. had some kind of a chart, either the Complete Chart or a language chart. About one-half of these were of an issue that made them of some service to the schools.

Any one who is at all familiar with this work must see that the schools are fatally defective in certain lines because they are not supplied with books and papers for the pupils to read, or charts, maps, globes and simple apparatus for illustrating the regular work.

While it is unwise to spend a large sum of money at any one time for material of this kind, yet it is the highest wisdom to buy some inexpensive helps which will give the schools an opportunity to do something outside and beyond what can be done with text-books alone. No school can do reasonably creditable work unless it is supplied with some of these things. Books are so cheap that a few may be furnished for each school at a small expense, and these may be passed from one school to another, and in this way all the pupils may have the benefit of all the books purchased by the town. Superintendents would render their schools a great service by purchasing cheap editions of the English classics instead of buying so many fourth, fifth and sixth readers. The expense would be much less to the town if this plan were followed and the opportunities for the pupils would be vastly increased.

It is hoped that this question will be carefully considered, and such steps taken as will remedy the evils which exist in these particulars.

GENERAL ITEMS.

These visits revealed some startling facts. In only two per cent. of the schools is instruction given in book-keeping; in four per cent. civics are studied; in about an equal per cent. instruction in music and drawing is given; in thirty-two per cent. map drawing is used, and in less than five per cent. an intelligent attempt is made to have the children learn something about plants, minerals and animals.

Teachers are required by law to give instruction in civics, and in physiology and hygiene, with special reference to the evil effects of alcohol and narcotics. It has come to be an accepted fact that instruction in music and drawing is necessary to the best work in the other branches. There are but few successful teachers who try to teach geography without using map-drawing to a greater or less extent; not the elaborate pictures, which were formerly made, consisting of shivering coast lines and delicately tinted political divisions, but an outline showing the boundaries, rivers, mountains and cities of the section studied, all of which may be drawn by the pupil in much less time than he could describe orally, what he indicates by his picture.

SUMMARY.

One has not enumerated all the evils found in the schools which are ranked as "poor" or "very poor" when he has reported that the teachers are deficient in education, ignorant of modern methods and lacking in personality. And one has not completed the list, when he has added to these serious charges the money spent in paying their salaries and the other expenses incident to maintaining the schools. Nor is the catalogue completed, when one has joined to all these items of expenses and to this list of horrors the fact that the children have wasted the most precious and susceptible years of their lives. The serious charge is found in the false ideas which children get of what a school should be, the bad habits which they form and the dwarfing, and in too many cases, the quenching of the student spirit in the child.

If a child has a teacher in whom he has confidence, for whom he has respect, and in whose presence he rejoices; if she unconsciously moulds and inspires him to do and to be something worthy, then the school makes it possible for the child to make the most of the best in him.

For these things not to be done means a failure more disastrous than many people can realize. For them to be done means a blessing richer than any lifetime of success can measure. These are matters of which the teacher, school officials and parents need to think and think seriously. For any of these parties to be responsible for these evils on the one hand is to be responsible for a crime. For all these parties to bring about the advantages which come from the other conditions is to do a work, the value of which can never be estimated.

The facts stated in connection with these visits to the rural schools of Maine may seem harsh to those who are not familiar with the conditions which exist in other states. But after visiting and studying the rural schools of five states, representing different sections of the Union, and two countries in Europe, it is only just to say that these criticisms apply with substantially equal force to those schools as to our own. This fact should not comfort or encourage us, but rather stimulate us to correct the evils which we find in our own communities.

THE AVERAGE OF THE PRESENT.

YARDS.

Sixty-five per cent. of the school buildings visited are located so near the road, and the yards are so small that the children are forced to use the public highway for play-grounds. Fifteen per cent. have yards from fifty to sixty feet square; ten per cent. have yards about one hundred feet square; five per cent. have still larger yards, and about five per cent. have no limits to their yards which the visitor could discover.

Not over five per cent. of all the yards are enclosed by suitable fences. In about the same number trees have been planted or flowers cultivated. It is evident to the most casual observer that in most cases the lots, on which school buildings have been erected, were selected without any special reference to their beauty or healthfulness; that the matter of size did not enter into the calculation in the selection of these lots, and the necessity or desirability of improving them seems to have been a matter of too small consequence to receive attention.

A brief study of this question ought to convince any one of the wisdom of selecting lots for school yards which are sightly, well drained and in every way adapted to the purpose for which they are used. They should be, if possible, two hundred feet square, and in no case less than one hundred twenty-five feet square, and they should be surrounded by fences of as durable a quality as the means of the town will permit. The people who form the community in the vicinity of the school should be urged to beautify them by planting trees, and the teachers and children should be induced to adorn them by cultivating flowers and shrubs.

These suggestions are made with the understanding that it will be impossible for many towns to make all these changes in any one year, but if the school officers will take the matter in hand, make the change in one neighborhood this year and another next, in a few years all the grounds will be put in such condition as will make them ornaments in the communities in which they are located, and a credit to the State. All must realize that this matter of making school yards attractive is one of no small importance, and that it may be of great assistance in training the children to love the beautiful in nature.

SCHOOL-HOUSES.

There is every indication that extensive repairs have been made on the school buildings within the last eighteen months. These improvements were seen in newly shingled roofs, freshly painted exteriors and interiors, and desks of a modern pattern. Inquiry developed the fact that many of these changes had been made within the time given above. This would seem to prove that the placing of the school property in the hands of the town has resulted in a marked improvement in the condition of the school buildings.

Taken as a whole, the school buildings are in a better condition than they were a few years ago.

All but two of the school-houses visited were built of wood. Twenty-one per cent. were ranked as in poor condition, sixty per cent. as fair, fifteen per cent. as good and four per cent. as excellent. Thirteen per cent. of these buildings were supplied with modern desks. Of those having plank desks, forty-seven per cent. were ranked as being in poor condition, thirty-two per cent. as fair, and twenty-one per cent. as good. In but two instances were the rooms visited listed as untidy. Sixty per cent. of the rooms were ranked as unattractive. In ninety per cent. of these it was noted that the teacher had done nothing to improve their condition.

But there are some things about these school buildings of which no one can approve. As has been already stated they are located too near the road and are in such a position that the dust sifts through the doors and windows, and the noise and confusion incident to travel disturb the school. In one case a building was found situated entirely within the limits of the road, being located between the fence and the traveled portion of the highway. All such conditions are harmful to any school and must prevent its doing the best work.

In only one instance was there evidence that any attempt had been made to place the windows at a proper distance from the floor, or to ventilate the room by any other means than by opening the doors and windows. The number, size and location of the windows, the distance of the bottom of the windows from the floor, the location of the stove, the system of ventilation and the arrangement of the seats are items which should receive intelligent treatment.

One would expect parents to be as careful of the eyes, comfort and health of their children as our best breeders are of their blooded stock. The construction and furnishings found in the average school-house, do not indicate that this is the fact.

One is shocked to see the vandalism that has been committed on so many school-houses. Clapboards have been removed, doors, windows and shutters have been broken, and desks, walls and ceiling have been defaced and mutilated. Everything that could be injured bears evidence of the polluting and destructive hand of the young or old barbarian.

Many of the school buildings are not provided with locks and but few of the windows are fastened, and there is every reason to believe that not a few are used as places of rendezvous by lawless characters.

The improvements which should be made in the condition of the school-houses must be made gradually because of the financial limitations of many of our towns. But it is true that all of the towns can do something in this direction each year, and if this plan is pursued, in a short time all the buildings will be put in good condition. There is no town in which the willful destruction of its property may not be prevented.

Since making these visits it has been decided to prepare plans for school-houses to be printed in the next report of this Department, together with some suggestions and explanations as to the matters referred to above.

CONDITION OF ROOMS.

In twelve per cent. of the schools visited the teachers had attempted to relieve the barrenness of their school-rooms by decorating them with drawings, engravings, charts, maps, leaves, flowers and other simple material which may be collected by any teacher who believes in the educational value of such decorations and has energy enough to prepare them. In some school-houses, which were rough board shells, the ceilings and walls were entirely covered with material devised and prepared by the teachers and children, and they were among the most attractive rooms visited, because of the artistic effects produced by a skillful use of nature and home made decorations. It is not easy to explain why all teachers do not do something in the line in which some have done so much.

Some of the school-rooms are dingy and barren beyond all possible description. The bare walls, the scarred and battered desks, the creaking and gaping floor, the broken backed stove pipe and the creosote stained chimney make up a combination which must be revolting to any child of ordinary susceptibilities. These masses of ugliness might be concealed by use of the means indicated above.

It is hoped that the time is not distant when the outside and inside of the school buildings will be painted in such tints as will be not only attractive but helpful to the eye. If but one of these things can be done, it is urged that the interior be painted in such a way as to relieve the children of the torture that must come from sitting in rooms which shock every instinct of refinement. The marked improvements which have evidently been made along these lines within a comparatively short time are a sufficient excuse for not pressing this matter further at this time.

OUTHOUSES.

The outbuildings of the average school-house in the rural sections of the State are a moral and physical menace to those

THE BEST OF THE PRESENT.

who have to use them. In many of them the windows have been removed, the doors are torn from their hinges, and in quite a number there are no partitions between the sections used by the boys and those assigned to the girls. All of them have the ordinary vaults and in most cases they have not been cleaned for years. The fearful odor which greets a person who is forced to go in the vicinity of one of these shanties, suggests conditions unpleasant to describe. But three outbuildings were found that could safely be called respectable.

The outbuildings of a school-house should be well built, with separate compartments for the boys and girls. The vault should be so arranged that it may be easily cleaned and this should be done at least twice each term. The building should be located in the rear of the lot and if it were surrounded with evergreens it would change a thing of hideous aspect to a comparative bower of beauty.

The condition of these hovels is so shocking that I feel justified in calling special attention, in strong language, to the duties of the towns in this connection.

DESKS.

About one-sixth of the school buildings are supplied with modern desks. The remaining five-sixths have the old-fashioned seats and these are marred and scarred by jack-knives and the experiences incident to the average rural school. It is gratifying to notice that in most school-houses, where new desks have been supplied, those of an improved pattern have been furnished, and it would seem that in a few years the old plank desk will be a thing of the past and that suitable seats will adorn all our school-rooms.

BOOKS.

The most of the schools are supplied with the regular text-books, although some were found where the committee had failed to furnish them in sufficient quantities. A few were supplied with books of a very inferior quality, but no general criticisms are called for in this direction.

It was noticed that as a rule the books were not properly cared for by the school authorities, by the teachers, or by the children. They were handled roughly, cut and marked promiscuously and there was practically no effort made to keep them clean, or preserve them from unnecessary wear and tear. But few of the school buildings were provided with cases for the protection of the books while not in use, and there was evidence that they were left on, or in the desks during vacations.

Each school building should be supplied with a substantial bookcase, with a strong lock, and the books should be placed in this receptacle during vacations. These precautions should be taken as a matter of economy.

PARENTS.

The time has come when parents must rise in their might and demand that qualified teachers shall be employed to take charge of the education of their children. They must not permit the teacher to do the work which should be done by the children. The parents must insist upon faithfulness, thoroughness in the work done, and regularity in attendance. They must bring such influences to bear as will convince school officials and teachers that they are thoroughly in earnest about these matters, and that no teacher can retain her position, with the approval of the patrons of the school, unless she is familiar with the facts which she is to teach, has some well considered methods of instruction, and is capable of compelling such work on the part of the children as will result in their growing in strength, knowledge and ability.

One is astonished at the extent to which parents are willing to remain ignorant of the schools which their children attend. In a large number of cases they seem to know little or nothing about the teacher, the work which their children are doing, or the way in which it is being done. One man was discovered who was unable to tell the name of the teacher who had charge of the school which his children attended. About eighty per cent. of the schools report that they have had no visits from parents for the purpose of learning what the work is, or assisting in making it more efficient.

One is at a loss to discover the reason for this apathy. Every intelligent parent must know that it will be a great advantage to his children if he visit the school, know the teacher and give her the benefit of his counsel. If parents would take the trouble to visit the school and inform the teachers in a truthful and proper way of the abilities, limitations and peculiarities of their children, they would be more than gratified with the results which would come from such conferences. The teacher is obliged to spend the most of the first term in stumbling upon the characteristics of the children whom she has to teach. She finds some shy, some forward; some who appear to be insolent and some who have every symptom of stubbornness. Some are prompt and proficient in their lessons and others are halting, stumbling and unsatisfactory in their work. Unaided, she must study out how much of these varying conditions are due to inheritance, or home training, and how much is caused by timidity, embarrassment, or excitement. All this information must be in the possession of the parents at the beginning of the term. If the teacher could have the benefit of it she could start with her work in a way that it is impossible for her to do under present conditions.

It is hoped that the good time is coming when parents will see the necessity of visiting the school, conferring with the teacher and being frank in their statements as to the abilities and deficiences of their children. The welfare of the school depends largely on their willingness to impute the best motives to the teacher for the corrections she finds it necessary to administer, and the methods she uses. If parents would invite teachers to their homes, treat them as persons in whom they have a personal interest and for whose work, at least, they entertain a high respect, the efficiency of the schools would be wonderfully increased.

As it is, parents are to a great extent either indifferent or hostile to the schools. Scathing criticisms are pronounced upon the teacher and her work, based often times entirely upon the reports made by children who have been angered, it may be, by wholesome restraint. The favorite child comes home with a complaint that he does not receive the assistance which he imagines he needs, or that he has been corrected for some misdemeanor, and at once the family take up the cudgels for the child against the teacher, all of which means a fatal injury to the school and the child.

It is for the interest of parents to give the teacher that cordial, hearty and unstinted support which will show the child that she has their confidence and respect. Without these helps the teacher is striving against fearful odds; with them she enters upon her work with an almost certain guaranty of success.

It hardly seems credible that parents are willing to allow their children to come under the instruction of a person of whose scholarship, character and training they know nothing. It is still more strange that they are willing that all these things should be true and still make no attempt to change this ignorance into definite information. It is the most strange of all that they cannot see that every interest which they have in their children lies in the direction of making the school the most useful that co-operation can render it. This cannot be accomplished until parents and teachers work in harmony for a common end; until each knows, appreciates, respects and sympathizes with the other; until the teacher has the full benefit of the knowledge and influence of the parent, and the parent feels that the teacher is the guide, director and friend of the child. When these conditions exist the common schools will be something vastly different from what we find them to-day.

In this work the responsibility rests largely with the parents. The teacher comes to the neighborhood a stranger, with

THE BEST OF THE PRESENT.

all the shyness of youth and inexperience. If acquaintances are to be formed, friendships are to be developed and the advantages which come from co-operation are to be enjoyed, the advances must be made by the parents. In many cases the teacher is a pilgrim and too frequently there is no one to take her in.

In the olden time the lawyer, the minister, and the teacher enjoyed a prestige in the community which is not accorded them at the present time. In losing this estimate of these characters we have lost much which would be of infinite benefit to those who accorded it and of vast encouragement to those who received it. The teacher's position is a responsible, dignified and useful one. All who are interested in the advancement and welfare of the community should recognize these facts and yield a cheerful tribute to those who occupy these positions.

It is impossible for one to give his best service if he feels that he has not the confidence and respect of the community for which he labors. One would not think of employing another to serve him and then seek in every possible way to cripple his power to work. This is what is practically done in many schools. It seems strange that parents cannot realize that these are facts. It will be stranger still if the time does not come, and come soon, when they will realize that they must act upon an entirely different line of policy if they are to be faithful guardians and honorable citizens.

SOME THOUGHTS BY THE WAY.

The highest function of the school is character building; not to succeed in this is to fail grievously. The teacher must help her pupils to see that hatred, jealousy, envy, untrustworthiness, and unkind words and acts injure, to an alarming extent, those who indulge in them; that one cannot cherish these feelings or do these things without being made miserable, and in time he must come to be small, mean and ignoble in thought, feeling and life; that he who is generous, kindly, sympathetic, glad in the successes of others, ready to add to their joys and eager to promote their prosperity, will receive a greater blessing than he bestows; that nothing reflects greater credit on one than an unwillingness to think or believe ill of others; that he is the best who believes and says the best of others; that a harsh judgment of others reveals much of malice and little of good in the one guilty of this offense; that gentleness, uprightness and thoughtful sympathy bring to their possessor the sweetest joys known to this life. They should learn that altruism results in happiness as selfishness must end in misery, and that no one can afford to spend in unworthy rivalries the strength which ought to be given to winning honest success. The true teacher will use every influence she commands to bring home to the hearts of her pupils these truths.

More study and effort should be given to developing the conscientiousness of the children. The controlling sentiment of the school should condemn the act of the wrong doer. We must so train the children that we can believe what they say, trust them alone, and have them feel that they are less than honest if their tasks are done for them. There is great danger of permanently injuring children by being consciences for them—by trying to decide all questions for them. We must not allow them to feel that we will direct them to the extent of always pointing out the right, and that by positive restraint we will prevent them from going far wrong. They must not feel justified in thinking that they are safe so long as they do not run against barriers which we have erected. To prevent these calamities we must cultivate in them the desire to decide the questions that arise in their experiences on their merits, and have the decisions and the carrying them into effect their voluntary act.

When the lives of great men are used to interest the children in what has been done in the world and to nurture in them worthy ideals, but little need be said about their having been presidents, or the battles they have fought, or the money they have accumulated, or the public honors they have received. With these things they will become familar without special effort on the part of the teacher. She should, however, make impressive the struggles, the triumphs over obstacles, the honesty, gentleness, purity, manliness, generosity, dignity and largeness of soul of the men studied. The deeds which these qualities make possible and that truly glorify history, and the thoughts which mirror the genius that gave them expression are most fascinating and helpful to children when properly presented. If the child's interest in these things can be enlisted, his respect, admiration and love for the pure is assured. If the teacher can make real to him the patience and faith of Columbus, the serenity and fortitude of Washington and the honesty and simplicity of Lincoln, she has accomplished a great work.

Teachers do not appreciate the good they can do by carefully preparing themselves to talk to their pupils on the topics on which they need instruction. Everyone is aware that there is too much talking, but most people are also conscious that there is but little effective talking. Ability to do a thing well comes to the average mortal because of practice and a sincere desire to excel. It is the duty of the teacher to select some subject that needs attention and so prepare herself that she can present to her pupils new ideas or old ideas in a new form. Striking forms of expression, apt illustrations and fresh facts contribute largely to one's success. These talks must not be too frequent, or at stated times or in any sense perfunctory. Do not fail, as you value your influence, to stop when you get through. Remember that brevity is not only the soul of wit, but it is a most effective form of emphasis. For a teacher to be able to say in well selected English and well turned sentences, and with a grace and force peculiarly her own, something that is worth the saying, is to possess a wonderful power for good over children.

The value of what a teacher does depends on what she is; her personalty teaches more than her words. Unless she helps to breed in the children worthy motives and ennobling ideals, she is a failure—absolute, ghastly. The desire to be worthy is worth more than glib recitations; the thirst for knowledge is more to be coveted than high ranks; a love for the best in literature and life is more fruitful than class honors, and the wish to do the right because it is right is more blessed than fantastic diplomas. The highest work of the school is to give such instruction, furnish such stimulus and form such habits as will help the child to be prompt to do justice, and alert in responding to the best within him. The motives that move him and the principles which govern him must come spontaneously from an honest heart.

Every lover of children must regret that there are so few teachers who realize that the great writers use language as a mirror in which to reveal the life of the past, the life of the present and the life that is to be; that the great painter uses color and form to place before the vision the same revelations. One who has any interest in knowing life must learn to interpret, to appreciate what the seers have revealed to us.

The historian writes the record of the past. The annalist and journalist write the record of the present. The poet writes the record of the future. We must study, ponder, estimate the work of the historian. We must read and sift the record of the journalist and the annalist. We must take in, as we take in the breath of life, the prophesies of the poet. It is life's greatest work to appreciate life. What the masters have given us furnishes food for the soul. Using this, life will be enlarged, made abundant. Without it, we are dwarfed, crippled, starved.

There is a larger number of people, than ever before, who have an honest concern for the betterment of the untrained classes of society. They desire to improve their condition socially; they seek to assist them to help themselves financially; they strive to train them intellectually. Their efforts are sometimes futile because of their hot haste to complete the reformation of the world during this year of grace. It

THE BEST OF THE PRESENT.

has taken the race many centuries to reach its present vantage ground. The best thing it has won during the journey is the strength which comes from experience. If we were made perfect in a minute, we should not have stiffening enough to hold us straight.

There are certain changes which must be made in the scope and character of the work done by the public schools if they are to receive the sympathetic and unstinted support of the public. These reforms are of such a nature that they can be most successfully wrought into the system by personal and local influences.

It ought to satisfy the ambition of any one, to be able to breed such a public sentiment in any community as would make it impossible for a superintendent or superintending school committee to refuse to furnish the schools with such English classics as will give the children an opportunity to read, and study, and know something of the masters of English undefiled.

If inexpensive reproductions of a few pictures of real merit and value could be placed on the walls of our country schoolrooms, and if the teachers could be so educated in these matters that they would come to enjoy and appreciate these things themselves, and if through this appreciation the children could be led to enjoy, appreciate and appropriate them, a greater work would be done for the children than can be done by any school which pursues the narrow policy of limiting the work of the children to text-books.

I earnestly hope that the time is not distant when some of the good people of the State who believe that visions of life and beauty are means of grace, will take these matters in hand, will give them the study which their merits demand, and will see that such steps are taken as will result in well ordered and beautiful school-yards, well built, well ventilated and well furnished school-houses, and will cause to be placed in the school-rooms such material as will enable the children to have intimate and appreciative acquaintance with some of the best things that the masters have given us in literature and in art. This is a field of labor in which all who seriously desire to do service to the young people of the State, have an interest.

STATE SCHOOL FUND.

There was apportioned to the cities, towns and plantations by the State for the year 1895, 518,185 70-100 dollars for the purpose of giving instruction in the public schools maintained by these municipalities. This is a large sum, when we take into consideration the population and valuation of Maine. The State should not shirk the responsibility of seeing that this money is expended in such a way as to do the greatest good. At the present time the State receives the money for the School Fund, apportions it to the different municipalities and with these perfunctory acts its duties and responsibilities seem to cease. This condition of affairs cannot continue without permitting a great wrong to the children.

The time has come when it is clearly the duty of the State, and one from which it should not shrink, to satisfy itself that this money is expended with a wise economy. It should know to whom it is paid, for what it is expended and should have some definite information as to the quality, character and training of those who have charge of the instruction of the youth who, a generation hence, are to be placed in control of all its interests. All thoughtful citizens realize that this money cannot be wisely spent unless it is used to pay for the services of competent, trained instructors. The State can, with a small expenditure of money, ascertain if her teachers possess these two essential requisites. The time has come when a Board of Examiners should be appointed, whose duty it shall be to provide for the examination of all persons who desire to teach. In some of the counties it would be necessary to hold but one examination each quarter; in others it would be better to hold examinations in two, three or four different towns. These examinatious should be held at such times as will give persons who desire to teach an opportunity to demonstrate their fitness to engage in the work. They should not be, at first, of such a nature as to eliminate from the profession a large number of those who are now teaching, but they should be of such a character as to prevent those who are grossly unfit for the work from remaining in the service, and should be of such increasing thoroughness that those who are but partially prepared for their duties will see the wisdom of more thorough preparation, or the necessity of leaving the profession.

The expenses of this Board could be paid many times from the saving which would come to the State in having an eligible list from which school officials shall select their teachers. The lowest estimate that can be fairly made of the incompetence of the teachers is that one-fifth of them are not qualified to fill the places which they occupy. This means that there are over one thousand teachers in the State whose education is so deficient as to render them failures as instructors. Assuming that these schools are in session only twenty weeks and admitting that they cost the towns only $150 each, for the full year, the aggregate sum paid for "keeping" these schools is $150,000. One needs to consider this question but a moment to realize that it is impossible for the State any longer to neglect, with safety, its duty in this matter. The issue is upon us; we must meet it. We must decide whether we will or will not be true to the trust committed to us.

It is not intended to imply that such examinations would eliminate all the incompetent teachers from our schools. It is believed they would make it impossible for a large proportion of those persons who are lacking in scholarship to receive authority to teach.

In the first place the most of the teachers who are not qualified to take charge of a school realize their unfitness and would not volunteer to be candidates for certificates. Some would be dropped because they could not secure certificates. The best would be retained and these would be made better by the study they would be induced to make to prepare themselves for their work.

This law would place in the hands of the State the power to say from what list of persons the teachers shall be selected. If towns desire to make more thorough examination of candidates for positions in their schools, the law should leave them free to do so. It should leave the matter of employing teachers and the management, discipline and everything connected with the general administration of the school in the control of the local authorities.

It must be apparent to all that the possession of a certificate from a State Board of Examiners would help to give the people of a community confidence in the scholarship and ability of the teacher placed over their children. This confidence has much to do with making a school successful. Without it but few teachers can succeed; with it a much larger number would do credit to themselves and render acceptable service to others.

COURSE OF STUDY.

It was, for a long time, a mooted question whether it was possible to prepare a course of study which could be used with profit in rural schools. This controversy has been decided in the affirmative, by the success with which the courses of study prepared for the cities have been used in their rural schools. Experience has made it clear that it is as easy to grade a rural as a city school. The only danger lies in making the divisions too numerous, and attempting too much in the way of details.

An outline course of study in which is stated simply and plainly the subjects to be taught, the order in which they are to be taken, the topics to be studied in each subject at a given time, cannot be otherwise than helpful to all who are connected with the school.

To have this outline in the hands of the teacher, with some suggestions as to the methods to be used, is to help to give definiteness and symmetry to the work. If these directions are followed with reasonable faithfulness the course must be of great service to the children.

THE BEST OF THE PRESENT.

To have a well considered plan of work, with some place at which to begin and some point for which to strive, is to set a goal before the children. These things contribute to systematic and hence to better work. They assist the teacher to ideas of what should be done, when it should be done and how it should be done. A course of study helps to convince teachers and children that they have something specific to do and when it is done, they have accomplished something. It helps to develop the feeling that they are held accountable for accomplishing a certain amount of work within a specified time, and this responsibility gives zest and develops enterprise.

A great many illustrations might be given of the evils resulting from the want of a course of study in our common schools. Perhaps a single experience will suffice. In one of the schools visited a child was found blundering through a selection in the sixth reader. The teacher was pronouncing about two-thirds of the words and it was evident the child had not the slightest idea of the thought expressed by the sentences she was trying to read. During the visit the same child appeared in the fourth reader class and stumbled through her work in substantially the same way as in the previous recitation. For work in arithmetic she was struggling with the mysteries of the addition tables. In answer to a question it was learned that the child was six years of age. This wretched condition of affairs was probably due to the fact that the child and her parents desired that she read in these books, she and they feeling that the size of the books used indicated the extent of her progress.

There can be no question in any one's mind but that a serious injury was done this child by the lack of intelligent direction of her studies. Had there been a course of study, backed by the authority of the superintending school committee and enforced by the instructions of the superintendent, it would have been impossible for this demoralizing condition of affairs to exist. The parents would not request it, the child would not expect it and the teacher would do what she knew should be done,—give the child such books to study as her advancement fitted her to use.

Perhaps this was the most ridiculous instance observed, still there were a large number of cases so closely approaching it in their general features that it could be substantially duplicated in many schools.

It is not expected that the course of study published in the appendix of this report will be followed literally, at first, in any school. It is hoped that superintendents and teachers will make it the basis of the work done. It is suggested that teachers begin, at once, to arrange their classes in five grades. It will be readily seen that the course is based upon the five readers used in most schools, one reader being assigned to each grade, the other work being so selected as to harmonize with this division of the studies. While it may not be desirable to limit the children, for the present, to the topics found in any given grade, it is best to commence immediately to work toward that end. If they are in advance in some branches and behind in others, give less attention to those in which they are specially proficient and more to the subjects in which they are deficient. By this plan of increasing the pressure in certain lines and devoting a little less time to other matters, it will be easy in a short time to have our rural schools as well graded as those in the cities.

School officials and teachers should not make the mistake of supposing that it is expected that they will use all of the books given in the list for "supplementary reading" in the several studies. These catalogues are made quite comprehensive with the hope that each teacher may find a few books that will prove peculiarly helpful to her and her pupils.

The teacher must study these books carefully to be able to use them skillfully. Unless she is, or grows to be, a student she cannot help her pupils to become students. The perfunctory reading of books is of little value. The reader must be helped to see, feel and think, for his reading to yield the highest return.

The tendency, in country schools, is to allow children to devote the most of their time to one or two studies. Such a method of work must result in a one-sided development. One child is fond of geography, another of arithmetic, another of history and another of language. This fondness is allowed to give direction and color to all their school work. While it is true that in the higher schools it may be safe to allow students some latitude in selecting their studies, it is not true that in the lower grades this permission should be granted. Children should be trained to read in such a way as to extract the pith from what is read and communicate these thoughts to others; they should have such a mastery of arithmetic as will enable them to use its principles and formulæ with intelligence, promptness and accuracy; they should be able to use their mother tongue with vigor and facility; they should know the important facts connected with the geography and history of their own town, state and country; they should be able to write a legible hand, and should receive such training as will enable them to conduct themselves easily in all the conventional relations of life. They should also receive such instruction as will help them to enjoy the beauties of literature, see the wonders of nature and appreciate the personality of the men and women who have made the progress of the world possible. In a word they should do such studying, receive such instruction and have such drill as will enable them to acquit themselves with credit in the social and business relations of life. A mastery of all the subjects required by the best common school courses of study indicates the minimum work that should be done by the boys and girls of a community that believes in rearing self-respecting citizens.

This course will not be of service to the schools of Maine unless it have the cordial and active support of the superintendents and teachers of the State. It will be necessary for them to study it, to understand it, and more than all they must know it well enough to adapt it intelligently to the needs of their particular schools. If these things are done there can be no question but that within five years all the schools of Maine will be doing substantially the same work along all the lines of study required by the statutes of the State. When this is done a pupil who is transferred from one town to another may continue his studies without loss of time.

If this course will help to bring about a fraction of the changes that it makes possible, the results will be of inestimable benefit to the children of the State. It is hoped that this matter will be taken in hand and that all concerned therein will give to it that support which will insure its largest success.

www.ingramcontent.com/pod-product-compliance
Lightning Source LLC
LaVergne TN
LVHW021426110826
845150LV00007B/2107

* 9 7 8 1 4 2 5 5 0 7 3 9 8 *